FIRST AMERICANS

The Blackfeet

DAVID C. KING

mc Marshall Cavendish
Benchmark
New York

ACKNOWLEDGMENTS

Series consultant: Raymond Bial

Marshall Cavendish Benchmark
99 White Plains Road
Tarrytown, New York 10591
www.marshallcavendish.us

Text, maps, and illustrations copyright © 2010 by Marshall Cavendish Corporation
Map illustrations by Rodica Prato
Craft illustrations by Chris Santoro

Library of Congress Cataloging-in-Publication Data
King, David C., 1963-
The Blackfeet / by David C. King.
p. cm. — (First Americans)
Includes bibliographical references and index.
Summary: "Provides comprehensive information on the background, lifestyle,
beliefs, and present-day lives of the Blackfeet people"—Provided by publisher.
ISBN 978-0-7614-4129-8
1. Siksika Indians—Juvenile literature. 2. Kainah Indians—Juvenile
literature. 3. Piegan Indains—Juvenile literature. I. Title.
E99.S54K56 2010
978.004'97352—dc22
2008041189

Front cover: A Blackfeet girl wears a red velvet trade cloth dress decorated with elk teeth.
Title page: A scrap metal sculpture marks the southern entrance to the Blackfeet Indian Reservation.
Photo research by: Connie Gardner
Cover photo by Marilyn Angel Wynn/NativeStock.com
The photographs in this book are used by permission and through the courtesy of: *AP Photos:* Karen
Nichols, 1; Tim Thompson, 40; *Getty Images:* George Catlin, 7; Hulton Archive, 30; *Alamy:* Interfoto
9, 10; Mira, 21; Rolf Hicker Photography, 34; Andre Jenny, 36; *Bridgeman Art Library:* Train
Passengers Shooting Buffalo for Sport c 1870. American School (19th century), 13; *Art Resource:*
Smithsonian American Art Museum, Washington, DC, 14; British Museum, 23; Werner Forman, 26;
Corbis: Hulton Deutsch Collection, 17; Bettmann, 38; *NatvieStock.com:* Marilyn Angel Wynn, 18, 19,
28; *The Image Works:* Werner Forman, 29; The Image Works Archives, 33.

Editor: Deborah Grahame
Publisher: Michelle Bisson
Art Director: Anahid Hamparian
Series Designer: Symon Chow

Printed in Malaysia
1 3 5 6 4 2

CONTENTS

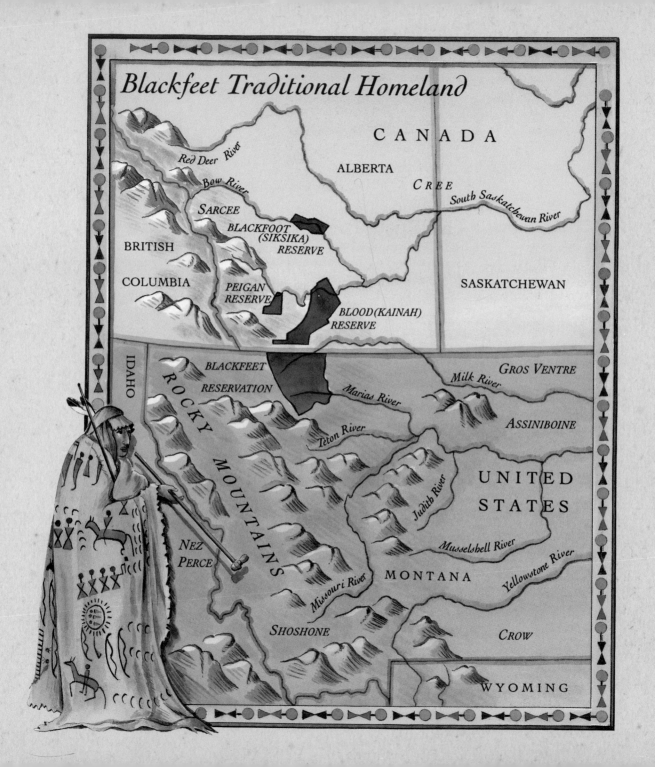

Blackfeet Traditional Homeland

CANADA

ALBERTA

CREE

BRITISH

COLUMBIA

SARCEE

BLACKFOOT (SIKSIKA) RESERVE

PEIGAN RESERVE

BLOOD (KAINAH) RESERVE

SASKATCHEWAN

Red Deer River

Bow River

South Saskatchewan River

IDAHO

ROCKY MOUNTAINS

BLACKFEET RESERVATION

Marias River

Milk River

GROS VENTRE

ASSINIBOINE

Teton River

NEZ PERCE

UNITED STATES

Judith River

Musselshell River

MONTANA

Yellowstone River

Missouri River

SHOSHONE

CROW

WYOMING

1 · THE PEOPLE OF THE BIG SKY COUNTRY

The Blackfeet Indians lived in the northern **Great Plains**—a huge area of grassland that once stretched more than 2,000 miles (3,219 kilometers) from Canada south to Texas. The Blackfeet, and other Plains Indians, shared these grasslands with millions of bison, the great shaggy beasts that provided the Indians with meat and with material to make homes, called **tipis**, robes, and dozens of tools and utensils.

Like some other Plains tribes, the Blackfeet moved often over their enormous territory to stay near the bison herds as they slowly migrated. That territory extended from the Saskatchewan River in what later became the Canadian Province of Alberta, south to the Yellowstone River in what is now Montana. In recent years the region has become known as Big Sky Country because of the canopy of deep blue sky

The traditional lands of the Blackfeet stretched from today's northwestern Montana north into Canada.

that extends from horizon to horizon.

Located on the eastern slopes of the Rocky Mountains, the Big Sky Country contains rugged hills, deep valleys, and scores of sparkling streams. The Great Plains to the south tend to be flatter and drier.

The Blackfeet consist of four tribes: the Northern Peigan (Pikuni), Blackfeet (Siksika), Kainai (formerly known as the Blood), who live in Canada, and the Southern Peigan (Pikuni), who live in Montana. All of the Blackfeet originally came from north of the Great Lakes. Europeans called them the Blackfeet because of the dark color of their moccasins. Slightly over half of the Blackfeet lived on the Canadian side of the border. The rest lived on the Montana side.

Until the 1700s the Blackfeet hunted bison, also known as buffalo, on foot. A family would form a band with several other families. One common hunting strategy was to force part of a bison herd to run over a cliff. Men disguised as animals and children waving blankets made the animals stampede. As the bison crashed to the base of the cliff, other

Artist George Catlin's 1832 painting showed hunters disguised as wolves moving in on a herd of bison.

hunters moved and killed the animals with short spears. The women were not far behind. They moved quickly to butcher the animals, knowing that the meat could rapidly spoil in the baking prairie heat.

Hunting bison this way was dangerous. But a successful hunt could supply the band with meat for weeks, as well as hide, fur, and bones to use for other needs. The Blackfeet preferred this way of life to that of growing crops, a way chosen by other tribes.

People of European background came to the Great Plains during the 1700s. Hunters, fur trappers, explorers, and then settlers came, bringing huge changes that would end the Blackfeet's traditional way of life forever.

In the early 1700s the Blackfeet were known as outstanding hunters and the most feared warriors on the northern Great Plains. But when the neighboring Shoshone acquired horses and used them to carry out several raids against the Blackfeet, it quickly became clear that warriors on foot were no match for those on horseback.

By the 1730s the Blackfeet, too, had horses, and within twenty years they had received guns from French and English traders. Horses now became part of the bison hunt, reducing the danger and turning the hunt into more of a sport. Most Blackfeet hunters preferred to use their short bows rather than guns. They could ride close to their prey and shoot four or five arrows in the time it took to fire a gun once and reload it for a second shot.

With horses and guns, the Blackfeet engaged in combat with

Blackfeet warriors lead two prisoners into camp. Normally the Blackfeet would rather capture a foe than kill him.

other tribes, a common activity among Plains Indians. Instead of large battles, small war parties made quick raids on an enemy camp, often capturing horses or taking prisoners. One major goal of warfare was to **count coup**. Instead of killing or wounding an enemy, the purpose was to get close enough to touch an enemy and escape safely. Counting coup was an important way to gain honor. A warrior could also count coup by capturing an enemy's horse or by rescuing another Blackfeet.

The Blackfeet might have benefited by the coming of the Europeans, with their useful tools, cloths, horses, guns, and other trade items. But other changes came with these strangers, and some of the results were tragic.

One of the most devastating developments was the spread of diseases, including smallpox, tuberculosis, measles, and

A Blackfeet medicine man uses his skills to treat a sick tribesman.

influenza. Over many centuries people in Europe had developed at least partial immunity to these diseases. Native Americans did not have this protection. From the 1600s on, epidemics periodically swept through one part of the Indian world and then another. A smallpox epidemic swept through Blackfeet lands in the late 1700s, destroying entire villages and killing an estimated 30 to 40 percent of the population.

Other developments in the nineteenth century also helped destroy the Blackfeet way of life. More and more Euro-American settlers pushed westward, hungry for farmland or searching for gold. Cowboys drove herds of cattle through the hunting grounds of Plains Indians, and the first transcontinental railroad cut across the migration paths of the bison herds. The railroad companies hired professional hunters to kill bison. Although some of this slaughter provided meat for railroad workers or hides to send to eastern tanneries, most of the animals killed were left to rot in the prairie sun.

Some U.S. government officials encouraged the slaughter, knowing that, without the bison, the Blackfeet and other tribes could not survive and would have to give up their traditional way of life. So the bison herds were destroyed. From an estimated thirty million bison in 1800, the animals were reduced to a few hundred by the 1880s.

The U.S. Army began to move in by 1850, building forts to protect settlers and forcing the Indian nations and tribes to move onto **reservations**—land set aside for the Indians to live on. The Blackfeet and other tribes resisted by fighting against the settlers and the army. But they were fighting against overwhelming numbers, and, with their food supply diminished, they had little hope of winning.

The fighting was brutal on both sides. Blackfeet warriors raided Euro-American settlements, killing indiscriminately. In an 1870 incident, the U.S. Army, searching for a band of hostile warriors led by Mountain Chief, encountered a peaceful band instead and killed more than two hundred, including women and children. In the meantime Mountain Chief escaped to Canada.

Reduced to poverty by the destruction of the bison, the

Train passengers shooting bison for sport. By 1890, the bison were close to extinction.

Blackfeet gave up. In 1877 the Canadian Blackfeet moved onto several **reserves** (the Canadian word for "reservations"), and in 1887 the Blackfeet in Montana signed the Sweetgrass Hills Treaty, defining the area of their reservation. From that time on, this proud people worked to preserve and restore the vital elements of their culture.

2 · THE BLACKFEET WAY OF LIFE

Blackfeet society was based on the family, and families were loosely organized into bands. Bands could be as small as nine or ten lodges with about eighty people, or as large as thirty lodges, with more than 250 men, women, and children. Each band had a chief, someone who commanded the respect of the people. A person could move to another band with related members quite easily, and marriage into another band was acceptable.

A small band formed a hunting group. For more than half the year the combined families lived the life of Great Plains buffalo hunters. In fact, until the Indians got horses, only those who lived in the north and the Cheyenne in the southern Great Plains followed the bison herds and then settled into winter camps. Until about 1700, other Plains tribes

A George Catlin portrait of a Blackfeet chief

relied on farming and hunted part of the time to add to their supply of food.

The Blackfeet hunting band camped within a short distance of a bison herd. When the herd moved in search of fresh grazing land, the Blackfeet packed up and followed. Their basic dwelling—the tipi—was easy to move. The sides—made of large pieces of buffalo hide—were removed. Two of the long poles that formed the cone-shaped frame were now attached to either side of a horse, with the other ends dragging on the ground. Shorter crosspieces for loading bundles completed the **travois**. A family could be ready to move in little over an hour.

The acquisition of horses changed both the tipi and the way it was moved. Before horses, the only animal the Indians had tamed was the dog. Dogs could pull a travois, but the load was much smaller. The diameter of a tipi was about 8 feet (2.43 meters) before horses and 15 feet (4.5 m) after horses were used.

The bison was central to the Blackfeet way of life. After a

A young girl has a comfortable place to ride—a litter tied to a travois pulled by her mother's horse.

successful hunt, there was excitement throughout the camp, because now there would be fresh meat for many days. As the women butchered a buffalo, they started with the choicest pieces—the hump ribs and the tongue. These were given to the hunters or to an ill or elderly person.

During the first days following a hunt, people enjoyed

Blackfeet women cut up bison meat, placing some on racks to dry.

roasting pieces of meat on a stick or cooking a larger piece of meat in a pit lined with hot stones. Some of the meat was cut in strips and placed on racks for drying in the sun or under a low fire, creating **jerky** that remained fresh and edible for several months. Another preserved food was **pemmican**. It was made by grinding the dried meat almost to a powder, then mixing it with berries and buffalo fat. Pemmican, which is still popular as a trail food, stays edible for a year or more.

The diet of buffalo meat was supplemented by a variety of wild foods. The hunters brought in other wild game, such as ducks and geese, turkeys, deer, and elk. Women and girls gathered wild fruits and berries, plus several kinds of root

The diet of Great Plains tribes was varied by the inclusion of edible bulbs, roots, and berries.

foods, including wild onions, potatoes, and carrots. These vegetables were often used to make a stew with buffalo meat, using a buffalo stomach as a cooking "bag," hung from a sturdy limb. On the Great Plains, where wood was scarce, flat dried pieces of bison dung, called "buffalo chips," were used for fuel.

Men raised and trained the horses, and taught their sons how to ride, then how to hunt on horseback. Girls also became skillful riders. When the band met with other groups for some special event, older boys stood guard over the horses.

Blackfeet Frybread

Frybread is a modern, pan-fried Indian food, which is enjoyed by Native Americans, including the Blackfeet, across the United States. The addition of the cinnamon/sugar mix and some blueberry jam can also add to the flavor. It is essential to have an adult help you.

You will need:

- 2 tablespoons (30 milliliters) sugar
- 2 tablespoons (30 ml) cinnamon
- 2 cups (500 ml) flour
- 2 teaspoons (10 ml) baking powder
- $1/2$ teaspoon (2.5 ml) salt
- 1 tablespoon (15 ml) cooking oil
- $3/4$ cup (175 ml) warm water, or more as needed
- cooking oil for frying

- measuring cup and spoons
- small bowl
- large mixing bowl
- mixing spoon
- small skillet
- 2 dinner forks
- serving plate
- paper towel

1. In a small bowl mix together the sugar and cinnamon. Blend well and set aside.

2. In a large mixing bowl, stir together the flour, baking powder, and salt.

3. Dust your fingers with a little flour to keep them from getting sticky. Add the cooking oil and the warm water.

4. Knead the dough with your fingers until it stretches but is not sticky.

5. Break off a piece of dough and form it into a ball a little larger than a ping-pong ball. Place the ball between your hands and stretch it out into a flat, thin pancake. This is not easy. If you have trouble, dust a flat surface and a rolling pin with a little flour and roll it out.

A young girl prepares frybread dough.

6. Punch a small hole in the center—this helps the bread fry evenly.

7. Ask the adult to fry the bread in about 2 inches (5 centimeters) of hot cooking oil. When one side is lightly browned, turn it over with two forks and brown the other side.

8. Place the cooked bread on a serving dish and cover it with a paper towel. Ask the adult to fry 2 or 3 more pieces. Sprinkle with the cinnamon/sugar mixture. Serve warm. Makes 8–10 pieces.

Boys learned most of the skills they needed by working with their fathers. They learned how to select the best wood for a bow, how to bend it to the right shape, and how to string it with twisted buffalo sinew to make a powerful weapon. Fathers also taught boys how to select perfectly straight branches for arrows, then how to attach a stone or iron arrowhead, using wet rawhide that would tighten as it dried.

In a similar way, Blackfeet women had set tasks and their daughters learned by working with them. One of their major tasks was to tan bison hide after skinning the animal and carving the meat. The hide was stretched on the ground and held in place with pegs. The women used scrapers to scrape the flesh off the hide. A series of washings and treatments, including one that involved rubbing the hide with the cooked brains of a bison, followed.

When the women and their daughters were finished, the hide was soft and flexible, and they used it to make leggings and shirts. Stiffer hide—or rawhide—was used to make items such as moccasins, drums, and shields. The Blackfeet, like all other Indian societies, liked to decorate their clothing with natural colors and dyed porcupine quills. After trade with Europeans began, brightly colored glass beads were used to make elaborate decorations. Dyes were used to paint scenes on tents, drums, shields, and many other surfaces.

This deerskin shirt belonged to Red Crow, chief of the Kainai, or Blood, tribe of the Blackfeet.

As cold arctic winds swept down into Alberta, the Blackfeet moved into sheltered mountain valleys for the winter months. They built more substantial lodges of poles covered with woven mats. Each band made its camp roughly a day's journey from its neighbors. They would move only if food or firewood was running low. Some bison also stayed in the valleys, where they had little room to maneuver, giving Blackfeet hunters a good chance to hunt them with bows and arrows.

Mini-Moccasin Guessing Game

Blackfeet Indians of all ages loved games, including simple guessing games. Especially during the winter months, when there was more leisure time, they would play these games for hours, never getting bored.

For this game, you will make three miniature moccasins, to hide a marble or coin in.

You will need:

* 3 sheets of paper (8½ x 11 inches or A4 size)
* scissors
* crayons or markers
* craft glue
* transparent tape
* 1 marble or coin

1. Fold one sheet of paper in half the long way. Round off the two top corners with scissors.

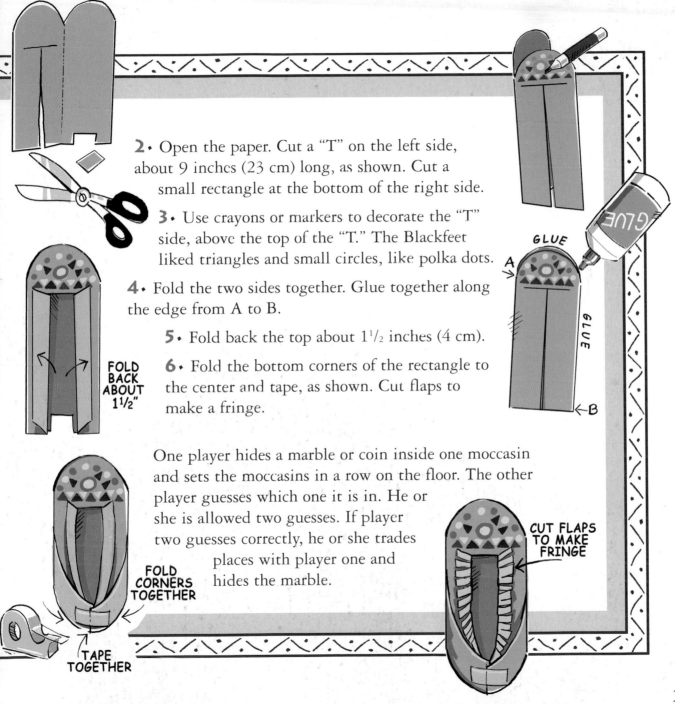

2. Open the paper. Cut a "T" on the left side, about 9 inches (23 cm) long, as shown. Cut a small rectangle at the bottom of the right side.

3. Use crayons or markers to decorate the "T" side, above the top of the "T." The Blackfeet liked triangles and small circles, like polka dots.

4. Fold the two sides together. Glue together along the edge from A to B.

5. Fold back the top about 1½ inches (4 cm).

6. Fold the bottom corners of the rectangle to the center and tape, as shown. Cut flaps to make a fringe.

One player hides a marble or coin inside one moccasin and sets the moccasins in a row on the floor. The other player guesses which one it is in. He or she is allowed two guesses. If player two guesses correctly, he or she trades places with player one and hides the marble.

GLUE

A

GLUE

B

FOLD BACK ABOUT 1½"

FOLD CORNERS TOGETHER

TAPE TOGETHER

CUT FLAPS TO MAKE FRINGE

3 · BELIEFS AND CEREMONIES

In midsummer on the northern Great Plains, the ripening of the purple **Saskatoon berries** meant that it was time for the Sun Dance. For two weeks hunting bison stopped and everyone headed for the site that had been selected for the Sun Dance. This was the only time all of the Blackfeet came together, which helped strengthen tribal unity.

Hundreds of tipis lined the banks of a small river. Boys tended the herds of horses, making sure they remained downstream from the camps to keep the water clean. Women and girls assembled the tipis and collected food for each band, while the men built a sacred Sun Dance Lodge. The centerpiece was a carefully selected cottonwood tree, forked at the top.

The purpose of the Sun Dance ceremonies was to thank the Great Spirit for the past year and to pray for the coming months of hunting and harvest. Like most Indian societies the Blackfeet

Chief Mountain in northern Montana was sacred to the Blackfeet, who used it as a place of meditation and coming-of-age spiritual quests.

A model of a Sun Dance lodge, showing male participants blowing whistles made of eagle bone

believed that everything, including places and objects, had a spirit, and individual tribal members might pray for special favors or give thanks. The prayers often took the form of dance and song. Another form of prayer involved seeking a vision from the spirit, usually by going through some form of ordeal, such as fasting.

One of the many elements of the ceremonies included painting symbols on a bison skull, then stuffing grass and sage in the eye and nose cavities. This served as a prayer for a good grazing year.

Another part of the ceremonies involved what were called

sacred bundles. A young man might receive a vision from the Great Spirit, or any lesser spirit, such as an animal, the moon, or some familiar object. In the vision the young man was told to collect and save specific things for their sacred power. The recipient also received permission to perform certain special rituals. Some bundles were owned by the entire tribe. Rituals involving these tribal bundles were believed to benefit all Blackfeet people by providing gifts of food or healing.

Some ceremonies involved painting symbols on a buffalo skull.

Toward the close of the ceremonies, a small number of volunteers agreed to subject themselves to a painful ritual known as the Sun Dance. The purpose was for the participant to receive a

The most painful moment of the Sun Dance ritual occurred when the participant felt the sticks begin to tear through his flesh.

special vision that would bring him unique benefits, and would also protect the tribe from future hardship.

The participant had skewers pushed through the skin of his chest muscles. Thongs stretched from the skewers to the fork of a cottonwood tree. As the participant leaned back, the thongs tightened and the skewers started to pull through his flesh, causing intense pain. The dancer—he was, officially, referred to as a dancer—displayed his courage by swaying back and forth to the rhythm of the drums. He might even defy the pain by singing or by blowing on a bone whistle. Finally his weight would force the skewers to tear through the skin, releasing the exhausted dancer.

The men who successfully completed the ordeal gained honor and respect. When the ceremonies were over, the bands went their separate ways and would not meet as a tribe again for another year.

In the 1890s, after the Blackfeet had been moved onto reservations, the U.S. government banned the Blackfeet Sun Dance. The Blackfeet managed to continue the ceremony secretly by including many traditional elements in their Fourth of July celebration. The tribe officially restored the Sun Dance in the 1970s.

The power of the vision sometimes led some to become **shamans**—healers who were often spiritual leaders, too. When a tribe member was ill, a shaman went to the person and performed special rituals and prayers designed to appease the spirits that were causing the illness. Shamans were often successful at healing because of their knowledge of medicinal herbs. Using yarrow to heal wounds, for example, or skunk-cabbage root for breathing problems, was the kind of knowledge that made some shamans famous. In the nineteenth century, many American pioneers turned to tribal healers to learn about the more than two hundred healing roots and herbs the shamans had discovered.

Geographic features in the Blackfeet country indicate the importance of the spirit world in their lives. The forest called Badger Two-Medicine in northwest Montana was a sacred place, which was frequently the site for the Sun Dance. A boy who was ready to become an adult was sent alone to Badger Two-Medicine on his **vision quest**. For several days he fasted and prayed, hoping to have a vision, perhaps of a bird or an animal, which would show that he was ready to be an adult member of the tribe, if approved by the elders.

Badger Two-Medicine was also where sweetgrass was harvested. Sweetgrass was believed to attract healthy spirits, especially during the Black-tailed Deer Dance.

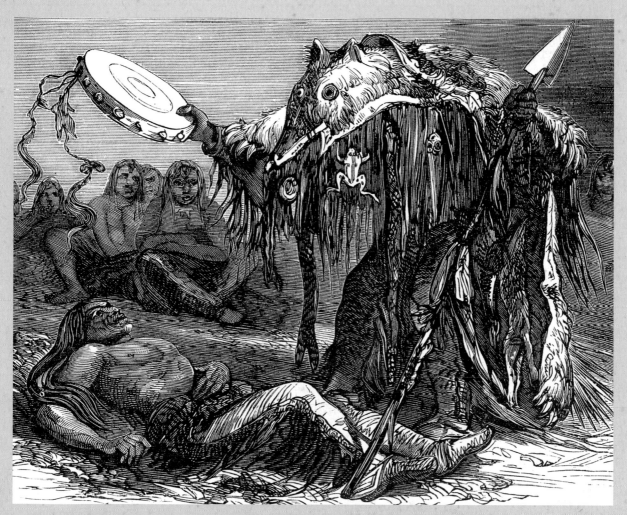

A Blackfeet medicine man works his magic on an ailing tribal member.

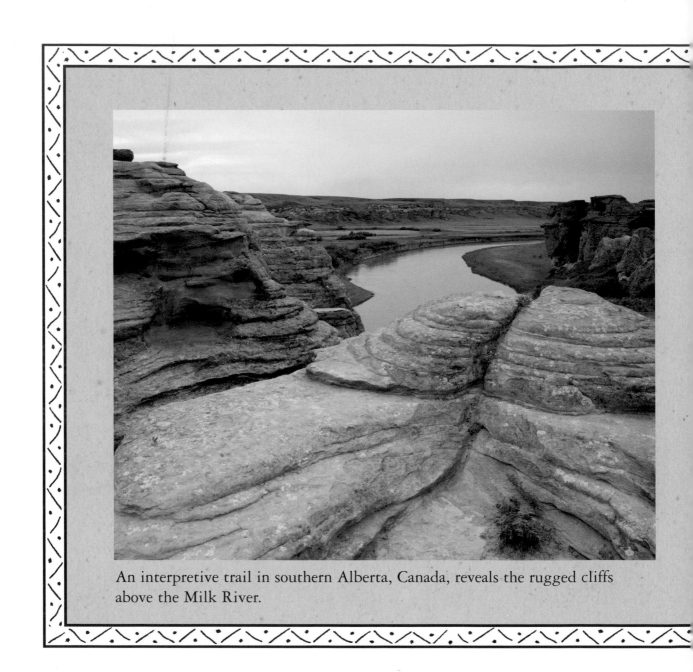

An interpretive trail in southern Alberta, Canada, reveals the rugged cliffs above the Milk River.

A Blackfeet Creation Story

The Old Man, as he was called, moved slowly from south to north, creating mountains, valleys, and forests as he passed along, and also making the birds and animals. When he grew tired from his labors, he would find a comfortable spot to lie down and rest. Many of these places are visible today. After he made the Milk River, for example, he crossed the river and found a place to lie down, marking out his position with stones. You can still see those rocks today. They show the shape of his body, legs, arms, and hair.

Another time, going north, he stumbled over a knoll and fell to his knees. To mark the spot he raised two large buttes and named them the Knees. They are called the Knees to this day.

The Old Man covered the plains with grass for the animals to eat. He marked off a piece of ground and in it made all kinds of roots and berries to grow: canna lily, carrots, turnips, bitterroot, cherries, plums, strawberries, and Saskatoon berries.

One day the Old Man decided to make a woman and a child. He formed them both—the woman and the child, her son—out of clay. After he molded the clay into human shape, he said to it, "You must be people. Arise and walk." They did so. They walked down to the river with their maker, and then he told them that his name was Napi—the Old Man.

4 · NEW BLACKFEET WAYS

The Blackfeet lost much of their traditional way of life in the late 1800s. The destruction of the great bison herds took away their livelihood, forcing them to move onto U.S. government–controlled reservations (called reserves in Canada). In addition, European diseases killed many Blackfeet, reducing the population to about 4,500 in Montana by 1900, with a few hundred more in Canada.

Reservation life was full of hardship and struggle. The people were totally dependent on the government for food and medical care. Dishonest government agents sometimes kept some of the Blackfeet's supplies to sell for their own profit. In the winter of 1883 no food supplies arrived at all and, over the next few weeks, more than six hundred Blackfeet died.

In the early years of the twentieth century, the U.S. government started a program called **assimilation**, persuading

A freight train rumbles across a valley floor on the Blackfeet Indian Reservation in Montana's East Glacier Park.

Girls wore uniforms to attend the Carlisle Indian School in nineteenth-century Pennsylvania.

Native Americans to give up their tribal ways and live like most white Americans. Many aspects of this program were hard on the Blackfeet. Children, for example, were taken from their homes and sent to government-operated boarding schools. They wore uniforms instead of their traditional clothing. Teaching was done in English only, and the children were not permitted to use their Algonquian language. They were taught that white-American culture was far superior to Indian cultures.

Still many Blackfeet refused to give up their culture. They continued to speak the Blackfeet language and taught it to their children whenever they could.

In the 1960s and 1970s many Indians became part of the civil rights movement, the struggle for equality for African Americans. Over the next forty years American Indians slowly regained some of what they had lost over the previous century. Some tribes and nations regained part of the lands they had lost. Others were awarded millions of dollars for mistreatment by the government and its agents, including the army. And still others opened bingo parlors and gambling casinos as a way to generate income.

The Blackfeet managed to build a successful economy on their reservation and the surrounding area. The reservation in Montana covers 1.5 million acres (607,000 hectares). It is bordered by Canada in the north and by Glacier National Park in the west. Of the roughly seven thousand Blackfeet living on the reservation, about half live by ranching and

At a Blackfeet school in Browning, Montana, students take turns being the teacher as each becomes fluent in some aspect of the Blackfeet language.

farming. The major crops are wheat, barley, and hay.

The rugged land of the reservation has 175 miles (281.5 km) of excellent streams. Outsiders are welcome to obtain tribal permits to fish the streams. The Blackfeet also make guides available to tourists. In addition the Blackfeet offer half-day and full-day tours of their reservation, which includes spectacular scenery and historic sites.

Visiting the Blackfeet

The Blackfeet Nation has taken steps to encourage all Americans, including other Native Americans, to learn about their beautiful land and culture:

- The Museum of the Plains Indian in Browning, Montana, features the creative work of many tribes of the northern Great Plains..
- North American Indian Days is held every year, with the Blackfeet Nation serving as host to Native Americans from throughout the United States and Canada. This festival includes contests in dancing and drumming. There is also a parade, the crowning of Miss Blackfeet, and a variety of foods and crafts.
- The Heart Butte Celebration is a four-day event held every August in the community of Heart Butte. It includes tours of new housing and a new school.

· TIME LINE

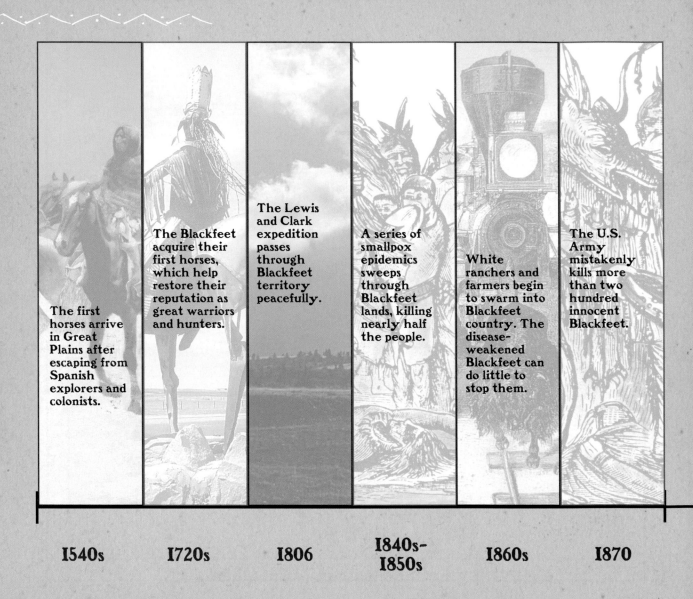

The first horses arrive in Great Plains after escaping from Spanish explorers and colonists.

The Blackfeet acquire their first horses, which help restore their reputation as great warriors and hunters.

The Lewis and Clark expedition passes through Blackfeet territory peacefully.

A series of smallpox epidemics sweeps through Blackfeet lands, killing nearly half the people.

White ranchers and farmers begin to swarm into Blackfeet country. The disease-weakened Blackfeet can do little to stop them.

The U.S. Army mistakenly kills more than two hundred innocent Blackfeet.

1540s   **1720s**   **1806**   **1840s–1850s**   **1860s**   **1870**

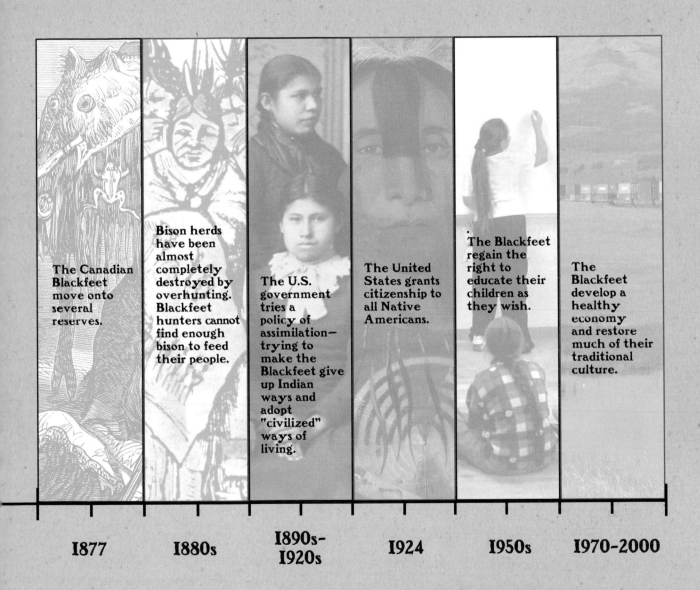

The Canadian Blackfeet move onto several reserves.

Bison herds have been almost completely destroyed by overhunting. Blackfeet hunters cannot find enough bison to feed their people.

The U.S. government tries a policy of assimilation—trying to make the Blackfeet give up Indian ways and adopt "civilized" ways of living.

The United States grants citizenship to all Native Americans.

The Blackfeet regain the right to educate their children as they wish.

The Blackfeet develop a healthy economy and restore much of their traditional culture.

1877

1880s

1890s-
1920s

1924

1950s

1970-2000

· GLOSSARY

assimilation: A U.S. government plan to have all Native Americans replace Indian ways with the ways of mainstream Americans.

counting coup: Getting close enough to an enemy to touch him and get away.

Great Plains: A huge area of grassland in the West of North America, stretching from southern Canada to Texas; it is home to huge herds of buffalo and wild horses.

jerky: Strips of buffalo meat dried by hanging in the sun or over a slow fire.

pemmican: Jerky that has been pounded into a powder and mixed with berries and melted buffalo fat to make a long-lasting trail food.

reservation: Land set aside by the U.S. government for American Indian tribes to live on, ending their freedom to roam.

reserve: The Canadian word for "reservation."

sacred bundles: Objects that had spiritual importance to Blackfeet individuals or the tribe.

Saskatoon berries: Purple berries common to the northern Great Plains; their ripening served as a signal to the Blackfeet that it was time for the Sun Dance celebration.

shaman: A medicine man or healer (sometimes a woman), important to practically all Indian tribes and nations.

tipi: A cone-shaped dwelling made of buffalo hides stretched over long poles; used by many Great Plains tribes, including the Blackfeet.

travois: A sledlike carrier made of two tipi poles tied to the shoulders of a horse or dog.

vision quest: The search for a "vision"—usually the spirit of an animal or bird, appearing in a dream—that will guide the individual.

• FIND OUT MORE

Books

Kalman, Bobbie. *Nations of the Plains*. New York: Crabtree Publishing Company, 2001.

King, David C. *First People: An Illustrated History of American Indians*. New York: DK Publishing, Inc., 2009.

Murdoch, David. *Eyewitness: North American Indian*. New York: DK Publishing, Inc., 2005.

Websites

General accounts of Blackfeet history and culture:

http://www.blackfeetnation.com/
http://indiannations.visitmt.com/blackfeet.shtn
http://www.nativeamericans.com/Blackfeet.htm

About the Author

David C. King is an award-winning author who has written more than seventy books for children and young adults, including *The Haida*, *The Huron*, *The Inuit*, *The Navajo*, *The Nez Perce*, *The Powhatan*, *The Seminole*, and *The Sioux* in the First Americans series. He and his wife, Sharon, live in the Berkshires at the junction of New York, Massachusetts, and Connecticut. Their travels have taken them through most of the United States.

· INDEX

Page numbers in **boldface** are illustrations.